VIEWPOINT

WORKBOOK

MICHAEL MCCARTHY
JEANNE MCCARTEN
HELEN SANDIFORD

CAMBRIDGE
UNIVERSITY PRESS

University Printing House, Cambridge CB2 8BS, United Kingdom

One Liberty Plaza, 20th Floor, New York, NY 10006, USA

477 Williamstown Road, Port Melbourne, VIC 3207, Australia

314–321, 3rd Floor, Plot 3, Splendor Forum, Jasola District Centre, New Delhi – 110025, India

79 Anson Road, #06–04/06, Singapore 079906

Cambridge University Press is part of the University of Cambridge.

It furthers the University's mission by disseminating knowledge in the pursuit of education, learning and research at the highest international levels of excellence.

www.cambridge.org
Information on this title: www.cambridge.org/9781107602786

First published 2012

Printed in Italy by Rotolito S.p.A.

A catalogue record for this publication is available from the British Library

ISBN 978-0-521-13186-5 Student's Book 1
ISBN 978-1-107-60151-2 Student's Book 1A
ISBN 978-1-107-60152-9 Student's Book 1B
ISBN 978-1-107-60277-9 Workbook 1
ISBN 978-1-107-60278-6 Workbook 1A
ISBN 978-1-107-60279-3 Workbook 1B
ISBN 978-1-107-60153-6 Teacher's Edition 1
ISBN 978-1-107-63988-1 Classroom Audio 1
ISBN 978-1-107-62978-3 Classware 1

Cambridge University Press has no responsibility for the persistence or accuracy of URLs for external or third-party internet websites referred to in this publication, and does not guarantee that any content on such websites is, or will remain, accurate or appropriate. Information regarding prices, travel timetables, and other factual information given in this work is correct at the time of first printing but Cambridge University Press does not guarantee the accuracy of such information thereafter.

Cover and interior design: Page 2, LLC
Layout/design services and photo research: Cenveo Publisher Services/Nesbitt Graphics, Inc.
Audio production: New York Audio Productions

Contents

Social networks

Lesson A Grammar Asking questions

A Complete the conversations with a correct form of the verbs given.

1. *A* ___Have___ you ever ___heard___ (hear) of speed-friending?

   B No, I haven't. What _____ (be) it?

   A Well, it's a bit like speed-dating, but it's just a way of meeting people.

   B Interesting. So, _____ you ever _____ (go) to a speed-friending event?

   A No. But I'm thinking of going to one. _____ you _____ (want) to go with me?

   B Um, no, thanks. But tell me how it goes!

2. *A* _____ I _____ (tell) you I went to a networking event last week?

   B No. What kind of networking event _____ (be) it?

   A It was for people who are looking for internships.

   B Oh, so _____ you _____ (look for) an internship right now?

   A Yeah. I'm trying to find one for the summer.

   B So _____ you _____ (make) any contacts at the event?

   A Yeah, actually, I did. I met some people from a software company.

About you

B Unscramble the questions. Then write answers that are true for you.

1. these days? / with / you / hanging out / are / Who

   Q: _____ A: _____

2. alone? / ever / Have / a weekend / spent / you

   Q: _____ A: _____

3. any of / you / call / Did / this morning? / your friends

   Q: _____ A: _____

4. in / Where / to / meet / you / people / go / your neighborhood? / can

   Q: _____ A: _____

5. your friends / you / all the time? / Do / text

   Q: _____ A: _____

6. outgoing / a kid? / Were / you / were / when / you

   Q: _____ A: _____

7. all your friends / joined / a social networking site? / Have

   Q: _____ A: _____

8. was / What / name / when / your / were / a kid? / best friend's / you

   Q: _____ A: _____

Lesson A Vocabulary Describing personality

A Complete the chart with the personality traits in the box.

aggressive	eccentric	narrow-minded	pushy	sensitive	thoughtful
annoying	intelligent	open-minded	relaxed	sweet	touchy
arrogant	laid-back	a pain	self-confident	talkative	weird

Generally positive	Generally negative	It depends . . .

B Complete the sentences with the words and expressions in Exercise A. Sometimes more than one option may be possible.

1. My boyfriend buys me flowers to say "thank you" and sends me cards to wish me luck. Yeah, he's very _____ and _____ .

2. My best friend's really smart. I mean, she's probably the most _____ person I know.

3. Most people love my uncle. He's very _____ . He'll chat to anybody about anything.

4. My brother was _____ as a child. He was always getting into trouble for pushing other kids on the playground.

5. One of my best friends can seem a bit _____ , like she thinks she's better than everybody else. I guess she's just _____ – you know, she's pretty sure of herself.

6. My girlfriend gets upset easily. She's pretty _____ .

7. My best friend never gets stressed about anything – you know, she's always _____ , even before exams.

8. My mom's the kind of person who's always willing to listen to other people's ideas – you know, she's really _____ .

9. One of my cousins is always bothering me. She's _____ and very _____ .

10. My neighbor has some very strong views and won't accept other people's opinions. He's so _____ !

About you

C Complete the sentences to make them true for you. Use the words and expressions in Exercise A, and any other expressions you know.

1. I can't stand people who are _____ .
2. If you want to be successful in business, you need to be _____ .
3. If you want to get along with people in general, you need to be _____ .
4. I really don't see myself as a/an _____ person.
5. I like to think of myself as _____ and _____ .
6. One of my best friends is so _____ and _____ .
7. I usually choose _____ and _____ people as friends.
8. I don't mind people who are _____ as long as they're _____ , too.

Lesson B Grammar Talking about habits

A Complete the sentences with a correct form of the verbs given.

1. My best friend can be really annoying. She _____ constantly _____ (look) at her phone. When we _____ (watch) a movie, she checks her email all the time. And when we're out together, she _____ always _____ (take) pictures of stuff. Then she _____ (post) the photos online. I mean, I'm usually pretty laid-back, but it's starting to drive me crazy.

2. My sister and I are actually really close, but we _____ (not call) each other very often. Occasionally we _____ (will / text) pictures to each other – or email stuff. But we're both so busy, we _____ (not answer) each other's emails unless it's really important. When she _____ (call), we _____ (talk) for hours.

3. I _____ (not waste) a lot of time online. You know, I _____ probably _____ (will / surf) the Internet for a couple of hours a day. But not all at once. I _____ (tend / take) about half an hour before work and probably half an hour at lunchtime to look at stuff online. And I _____ (email) people at night. But a lot of my friends _____ (will / stay) online for hours and hours.

B Circle the best option to complete the conversations.

1. *A* How many times a day do you text your friends?

   B Well, **I'll send / I'm sending** a reply whenever I get a message. So, I don't know – maybe 20 or 30 times a day. Mostly, **we make / we're making** plans by text. But **I tend to call / I'm calling** if I want to have a real conversation or something.

2. *A* How do you keep in touch with your family when you're away from home?

   B When **I'll travel / I'm traveling**, we try to video-chat on the Internet. That way we can talk for free. And **we'll email / we're emailing**, too. I like to keep in touch.

3. *A* Have you ever used the Internet to find a friend?

   B Yeah. **I'm searching / I'm always searching** online to see if I can find my old school friends. **I'll find / I'm finding** someone every once in a while. It's fun to see what they're doing now. Occasionally **I'll contact / I'm contacting** them. But **I don't do / I'm not doing** it often.

About you

C Now write your own answers to the questions in Exercise B.

1. _____

   _____

2. _____

   _____

3. _____

   _____

Lesson C Conversation strategies

A Read the conversations. Circle the appropriate follow-up questions.

1. *A* How do you usually keep in touch with your friends back home?

   B How do we keep in touch? We tend to text. Or we'll check each other's profile pages.

   A **And do you ever call each other? / And you never keep in touch with them?**

   B Yeah. Sometimes.

2. *A* So, yeah, Mark and I have been dating for ten months now.

   B That's great. **But you lost touch, right? / So, you're getting along well?**

   A Yeah. It's great. He's so thoughtful and just a really cool guy.

3. *A* My parents got divorced when I was little.

   B That's too bad. That must have been hard.

   A Yeah, but my mom remarried, and my stepdad's great. He's really cool.

   B That's good. **But you don't see your mom, right? / So you do a lot together?**

   A Yeah. We always hang out as a family.

B Read the conversations. Write the appropriate follow-up question for each conversation. There are two extra questions.

> a. And does he know you at all?
> b. And how often do you see them?
> c. But would you feel sad?
> d. But you wouldn't tell them, right?
> e. So you didn't talk to each other at all?

1. *A* How would you feel if you lost touch with a good friend?

   B It depends. It happens sometimes.

   A _____

   B I guess so. Again, it depends.

2. *A* Have you ever had a fight with a friend over something silly?

   B Yeah, once. My friend Jack and I had an argument about this girl. We didn't speak for weeks.

   A _____

   B No, not a word.

3. *A* Have you always had a lot of friends or just one or two close friends?

   B I tend to have one or two close friends. I don't have a big circle of friends.

   A _____

   B Oh, we hang out pretty often, like once or twice during the week and then every weekend.

Lesson D Reading Personal profiles

A **Prepare** Circle two facts and underline three pieces of advice. Who is this information for – employers or candidates?

Getting the most from online profiles

1   Over 30 percent of employers say they currently use, or plan to use, social networking sites to obtain information about job candidates. However, only 16 percent of workers write their online profiles with potential employers in mind.

2   What may be more worrying for today's job seekers is that 34 percent of managers said they have rejected a candidate because of the information they obtained online. Finding inappropriate photographs is one of the main reasons for rejection.

3   This trend of using social networking sites as an employment tool is growing. "We can learn a lot about a candidate from his or her online profile," says Mindy Watson, director of human resources at an advertising agency. "We want to see if the person will fit in well at our company, so the information in an online profile is valuable to us."

4   Hiring managers also tend to use social networking sites when they are looking for new hires. So if you want to use your profile to find a new job either now or in the future, here are some do's and don'ts.

5 ➤ ☐   Keep your profile up to date, even if you are not looking for a job. Make sure you list your latest achievements. Hiring managers are looking for the best people for their companies, so make sure that you present yourself in a positive way. You never know – someone may invite you to come in for an interview even before you start looking for a new job.

6 ➤ ☐   It is always best to avoid making any negative comments about your current or previous boss, company, or co-workers. If employers think that you will damage their image after you leave the company, they won't want to hire you.

7 ➤ ☐   If you are always telling off-color jokes or joining weird or silly groups, be careful. One of the fun things about networking sites is that you can connect with other people who share your sense of humor. However, these groups don't always leave a potential employer with a good impression. Instead, be selective and join groups that demonstrate your professional goals or social involvement. This shows you are thoughtful and creates a positive online image.

8 ➤ ☐   Be careful also if you are trying to hide your job search from your current boss. One of your co-workers might see your profile and mention it. You could find that your boss withholds that promotion or raise you were expecting. However, if your boss does find out and accuses you of looking for a new job, don't deny it. It is better to tell the truth than risk a negative reference.

9 ➤ ☐   Remember that other people will see the contacts you have made if you don't keep your friends list private. So in addition to keeping your friends' inappropriate pictures and comments off your profile, be cautious about who your online friends are.

10 ➤ ☐   Review the pictures you have uploaded to your profile, the personal information you have given, and any blogs or sites you have linked to. Delete anything you might regret later.

11   Always bear in mind that employers can use your social networking profile to evaluate you, so show self-confidence (without being arrogant) and promote yourself well. Think of it as a face-to-face meeting with an employer, and present the image of yourself that you want to promote.

B Information flow **Where do these headings fit in the article? Write the letters a–f in the boxes in the article.**

    a. Don't badmouth your current or previous employer

    b. Don't forget: Others can see your friends

    c. Don't mention your job search if you are still employed

    d. Do join groups . . . selectively

    e. Do update your profile regularly

    f. Do clean up your "digital dirt"

C Read for detail **Are the sentences true or false, or is the information not given in the article? Write T, F, or NG. Correct the false sentences.**

1. Companies use social networking sites to obtain information about their employees' family life. _____

2. Your online profile can get you a job, even if you're not looking for one. _____

3. It's a good idea to show your sense of humor in your profile. _____

4. If your boss finds out about your job search, you should deny it. _____

5. You can get fired from your current job because of your online profile. _____

6. When you're looking for a job, it matters who your online friends are. _____

7. It's fine to be arrogant in your profile, if you're promoting yourself. _____

8. When you write a profile, you should imagine you're talking to an employer. _____

D Focus on vocabulary **Replace the words in bold with the verbs and expressions from the article.**

    obtain

1. Employers **get** information about candidates from their online profiles. (para. 1)

2. One reason employers have **not hired** candidates is because of inappropriate photos. (para. 2)

3. Your boss might **not give you** a promotion if he or she knows you are looking for a job. (para. 8)

4. If your boss **says you're** looking for another job, don't **say you aren't doing** it. (para. 8)

5. Don't post anything you'll **be sorry about** later. (para. 10)

6. The best way to **show people your good qualities** is to have a clean profile. (para. 11)

E **Write a response to each of the sentences in Exercise D. Use the verbs and expressions from the article.**

1. I think this happens all the time. When I applied for a job, they obtained information about me from my online profile.

_____

2. _____

3. _____

4. _____

5. _____

6. _____

Writing A script for an online debate

A Read the debate script. Circle the correct words to show contrasting ideas.

Social networks – a waste of time or a good way to find a job?

Some people believe that social networks are a waste of time. **However, / On the one hand,** other people enjoy using them to keep in touch with friends and family. **While / On the one hand,** it is fun to have an online profile and share news and photographs with people you know. **On the other hand, / Whereas** it is important to realize that employers can use your profile to see if they want to hire you. **While / However,** you might think your pictures are harmless, employers might not agree. If you have a profile on a social networking site, make sure you promote a professional image. In conclusion, it is better to keep your profile up to date with appropriate content, or it might cost you your dream job.

Help note: *Contrasting ideas*

However, and *On the other hand,* contrast the ideas in a previous sentence with the ideas in a new sentence.

While and *whereas* contrast ideas within one sentence.

In sentences with *while* and *whereas*, use a comma at the end of the first clause.

B **Editing** Read the Help note. Then correct the mistakes in these extracts from scripts. Change the expression, or the punctuation, or both. There is more than one correct answer.

1. You might think your party photos are harmless. **Whereas** employers might see them in a different way. You might think your party photos are harmless. However, employers might see them in a different way.

2. Some people never put photos on their profiles **on the other hand** other people post a lot of pictures. _____

3. Job seekers are not cleaning up their profiles **however** employers are checking them. _____

4. **However** an online profile may be public, it is not fair to use it to reject a job candidate. _____

5. **While** I understand why employers check people's profiles online. Personal profiles are not meant for employers. _____

6. You can control who sees your résumé **however** you can't always control who has access to your online profile. _____

C Write a script for the debate in Exercise A. Include an introduction, contrasting ideas, and a conclusion. Then check your script for errors.

These days everyone uses social networking sites, and job seekers are using them to promote themselves to potential employers. While you might think your personal profile is private, ...

Listening extra   Keeping in touch

A   Check (✔) the expressions that describe ending relationships.

☐ break up with   ☐ get engaged   ☐ make friends
☐ fall out with   ☐ get married   ☐ separate
☐ get divorced   ☐ lose touch with   ☐ "unfriend"

B   🔽 Listen to four people talk about relationships. Answer the questions. Write the names. There is one extra question.

Andrea   Nuray   Oscar   Christa

1. Who would never contact someone from a previous relationship? _____
2. Who "unfriends" people occasionally? _____
3. Who is getting divorced soon? _____
4. Who lost touch with someone over a period of time? _____
5. Who just got back in touch with someone after a long time? _____

C   🔽 Listen again. Are the sentences true or false? Write T or F. Correct the false sentences.

Andrea

1. Andrea and her roommate stopped calling because they had an argument. _____
2. They only keep in touch on special occasions. _____

Nuray

3. Nuray likes to know what her old friends are doing every day. _____
4. Sometimes she'll contact her old boyfriends online. _____

Oscar

5. Oscar has too many friends to keep in touch with. _____
6. He gets upset when he reads mean comments on his profile. _____

Christa

7. Christa's life has changed a lot in the last ten years. _____
8. She finds it difficult to keep in touch with her husband when she's traveling. _____

D   🔽 Listen again to the last thing each person says. Do you agree or disagree? Write a sentence expressing your views.

1. _____

2. _____

3. _____

4. _____

The media

Lesson A Grammar Adding information

A **Is the information in bold essential, or is it extra? Write D (defining, or essential) or N (non-defining, or extra). Then add commas where necessary.**

1. I can't stand magazines **that are full of ads**. _____

2. Fashion magazines **which are really mostly about shopping** usually have the most ads. _____

3. The celebrities **who are always in the gossip magazines** don't really interest me. _____

4. Good theater actors **who never get as famous as movie actors** deserve more attention. _____

5. I really enjoy reading about celebrities and the charity work **they do**. _____

6. When I buy music magazines, I'll usually buy the ones **which have a free CD**. _____

7. The magazine **I like the most** is about art and culture. _____

B **Complete the conversations with *who*, *that*, or *which*. If you can leave them out, write parentheses ( ) around them. Sometimes there is more than one correct answer.**

1. *A* I'm looking for a good TV show _____ could help me improve my listening skills in English. What do you think I should watch?

   B I think maybe sitcoms, _____ are often about everyday life, are best for that. Check out the two _____ I watch – Wednesday nights at 8:00 and 8:30 on Channel 2.

2. *A* Look at this magazine _____ I just bought . . . it's full of ads! Why can't I find magazines _____ aren't trying to sell me stuff?

   B Well, magazines have to make money, _____ ads provide.

3. *A* Ugh, I can't listen to any more about that actress, Leya March, _____ seems to be on the news every minute of the day!

   B Oh, I find it all pretty entertaining. And most of the events _____ are happening in the world are pretty depressing, so hearing about her is kind of a relief.

4. *A* I'm obsessed with reality shows. The people _____ are on them are hilarious.

   B I know. They'll do anything to be famous, _____ can be so funny to watch.

C **Complete the sentences with relative clauses using *who*, *that*, or *which* and the information in parentheses. Add commas where necessary.**

1. The TV show _____ is about a group of college students. (I like it best of all.)

2. My best friend _____ has a TV in every room. (She watches TV constantly.)

3. The online magazine _____ is about current events. (I read it the most.)

4. I watch TV every night to relax _____ . (I need to do that before I go to bed.)

5. Some people are obsessed with celebrity gossip _____ . (I think it's ridiculous.)

Lesson B Vocabulary Describing research

A Circle the correct prepositions to complete the sentences.

1. There is a lot of concern **about / on / of** violence on TV.
2. Research has shown that exposure to violent TV shows has an effect **to / on / with** the brain.
3. One reason **for / between / of** lower test scores is that kids spend more time on the Internet.
4. We don't know enough about the impact of TV **in / on / with** the youngest children.
5. Many of the ads on TV **between / on / for** junk food are aimed at children.
6. The rise **in / on / with** Internet advertising may affect young people's habits, too.
7. Scientists don't know all the causes **of / with / about** obesity in young people.
8. There may be a relationship **on / with / between** watching TV and language development.

B Complete the blog post with the words in the box. Sometimes more than one answer is possible.

concern	impact	increase	influence	link	✔ problem	research

Is there a problem with TV?

Some researchers believe that watching TV has a huge _____ on children. Some experts claim that they have found a _____ between watching TV and learning problems in children. However, people don't have the same _____ about educational TV shows. It's my feeling that we should look at their _____ on children, too. While it's likely that some educational shows are good for children, what's disturbing is that there has been a large _____ in advertising for fast food and other junk food during these programs. I believe these commercials contribute to unhealthy eating habits. So before I make a decision about TV for my kids, I need to know more. What I'm saying is, we need more _____ on this subject.

Posted by Blog Girl, March 3

(tablet sidebar: Settings, Browse, Channels, Home, Menu)

About you

C Answer the questions with your own opinions.

1. Do you think watching TV has an impact on your own behavior? Why or why not?
   _____

2. Do you have any concerns about young children and TV?
   _____

3. Why do you think there is a relationship between watching TV and obesity in young people?
   _____

4. Do you think watching TV is the main cause of poor test results? Why or why not?
   _____

Lesson B Grammar Linking ideas

A Complete the information about TV viewing. Use *that* or the correct form of *be + that*.

How much TV do you watch every week? You may think _____ you watch too much TV. But what's surprising about today's TV shows _____ they might actually help your brain. It's probably true _____ many people watch shows with no real benefit. However, some experts now claim _____ TV shows today are more advanced than ever. One key difference _____ they have more complex stories. Experts claim _____ the brain has to work harder to understand them. So next time you want to watch TV, don't feel guilty! Go ahead and turn it on. It just might be making you smarter.

B Rewrite the sentences using a *that* clause. Start with the words given in parentheses, and add a verb where necessary.

1. TV and the Internet have changed children's reading habits. (Some experts . . .)

   Some experts agree that TV and the Internet have changed children's reading habits.

2. Many children prefer watching TV to reading. (What's clear . . .)

   _____

3. Reading improves children's vocabulary development. (One problem with spending less time reading . . .)

   _____

4. Most books and magazines will only be online in the future. (It's likely . . .)

   _____

5. Publishers may stop printing books altogether. (What's interesting . . .)

   _____

6. Going digital is inevitable. (Many people believe . . .)

   _____

About you

C Complete the sentences with your own ideas about the impact of TV and the Internet.

1. It's not surprising _____ .

2. Many people feel _____ .

3. What's clear is _____ .

4. It's possible _____ .

5. One problem with the Internet is _____ .

6. It's true _____ .

Lesson C Conversation strategies

A Complete the conversation with the *which* comments in the box. There is one extra.

which always ends up being expensive	which is so annoying
which is not surprising	which totally goes against what I just said

Marco I really hate getting junk email.

Lina Me, too. Like those email chains people send. There's one I've seen at least ten times.

Marco _____ .

Lina I know. Some of them are so stupid.

Marco Wait, though. Somebody sent me a video clip a couple of days ago. Hold on, you have to see
this – _____ .

Lina Um, OK . . .

Marco Oh. They must have taken it off. It's not here anymore.

Lina _____ . Happens all the time –
you finally find a good one, and it's gone.

B Complete the conversations with *You know what . . . ?* Use the information in parentheses.

1. *A* Video ads are all over the place. It's so annoying.

   B You know what really gets me? They're in your personal email. (It really gets me.)

2. *A* Check this out – do you know about this video site? It's awesome.

   B Yeah, it's great. And _____ I'm totally
addicted to it. (It's ridiculous.)

3. *A* My friend's constantly posting videos and pictures of me without asking.

   B _____ When you start looking for a
job, employers can see those pictures and videos. (I'd be concerned about this.)

C Complete the conversations with the expressions in the box.

just so annoying	I prefer	really bothers me
really scares me	so convenient	so important

1. *A* You know what _____ ? You can't watch a video clip on this website without
watching an ad first. And you can't skip it!

   B Which is _____ . There should be a way to get past it.

2. *A* Are you still watching DVDs on your laptop?

   B Yeah. I can take them with me when I travel, which is _____ .

   A It is. But you know what _____ ? Just downloading them off the Internet.

3. *A* I finally figured out how to add privacy controls to my profile.

   B Which is _____ , especially now that you're looking for a job.

   A Yeah, but you know what _____ ? My friends who *don't* use privacy controls.

Lesson D Reading Distractions

A Prepare If something is *distracting*, it takes your attention away from what you're doing. Think of three distractions – things that you find distracting – in your daily life.

B Read for main ideas Read the article. Does the writer mention any of the distractions you thought of in Exercise A?

DISTRACTIONS: Should we be concerned?

1 Young people have always been faced with distractions, but now with computers, video games, tablets, and smart phones, there are even more things demanding their attention. A recent study found that more than half of students – aged 8 to 18 – are distracted while doing homework, and for 56 percent of the time they are also using the Internet, watching TV, or using some other form of media. Should we be concerned about these kinds of distractions?

2 Some researchers say that one problem with these technologies is that they have a greater impact on young people. First, young people's brains become used to constantly switching tasks, which makes them less able to pay attention for long periods of time. Second, some experts say that distraction has an impact on people's ability to think deeply.

3 One study looked at the computer use of students in grades 5 through 8. The researchers found a link between access to home computers and a drop in reading and math scores. What is clear, they say, is that middle graders are mostly using computers to socialize and play games rather than for educational purposes. The study used data from 2000 to 2005, before the huge rise in social networking sites, so the problem may be even more extreme today.

4 In other studies, researchers have shown that boys who have access to video game systems at home are frequently distracted from their homework. The research showed that the boys' reading and writing scores suffered as a result. It's also possible that playing video games, which involves multitasking (doing more than one thing at a time) has more impact on the brain than distractions such as watching TV. In one study, boys aged 12 to 14 spent an hour every other night playing video games after they finished their homework. On the other evenings, they spent an hour watching a movie on TV. The researchers found that on nights when the boys watched TV, they slept better than when they played video games. The video games also had a negative impact on the boys' ability to remember vocabulary, even words that they were already familiar with.

5 What kinds of activities, then, should we encourage children to do? Some scientists say that reading books is a good choice because children are less distracted when they read books. This may be because children identify with the characters and are able to focus their attention for longer periods of time. Many studies have found that students who read books have significantly higher test scores than students who don't.

6 On the other hand, critics of these studies claim that playing complex computer games and doing Internet searches actually improve a person's ability to concentrate and stay focused. They say that books promote one type of learning, whereas the Internet promotes a different, equally beneficial type.

7 The impact of computer use on the brain is a complex issue, and not all experts agree on its positive and negative effects. What is clear is that electronic media are here to stay. For this reason, education experts may need to turn their attention to designing educational technology that helps students focus on learning and not be distracted by the media they are using.

C **Understanding viewpoints** Check (✔) the points that the writer makes in the article.

☐ 1. Many children are being distracted by electronic media while they are doing homework.

☐ 2. Some distractions can be more harmful than others.

☐ 3. Watching a movie has a more positive effect on the brain than doing activities that involve multitasking.

☐ 4. Children who read books do well in all of their school subjects.

☐ 5. Experts all agree that technology has negative effects.

D **Read for detail** Circle the correct information to make true sentences about the article.

1. According to the article, various technologies distract children because **young learners think they're fun / the user has to constantly switch tasks**.

2. The article suggests that **watching TV / playing video games** is a form of multitasking.

3. One study showed that **TV / video games** had a more negative impact on young boys' sleep.

4. This study also showed that **watching TV / playing video games** had an effect on the boys' ability to remember vocabulary.

5. The study in which researchers found a link between home computers and lower test scores used information from **before / after** the huge rise in social networking.

6. **Critics / Supporters** of these studies say playing video games and surfing the Internet actually improve people's ability to concentrate.

7. The writer suggests that educational researchers should be focusing on improving online materials because electronic media **are better than books / aren't going to disappear**.

E **Focus on vocabulary** Find these words and expressions in the text. Match them with their meanings. Write the letters a–f.

1. extreme (para. 3) _____   a. start looking at

2. be familiar with (para. 4) _____   b. people who don't like an idea

3. identify with (para. 5) _____   c. know

4. critics of (para. 6) _____   d. feel a connection with

5. a complex issue (para. 7) _____   e. a difficult subject

6. turn attention to (para. 7) _____   f. very great

F Do you think that technology has a positive or negative impact on your ability to study? Give reasons for your answer.

_____

_____

_____

_____

_____

_____

_____

Writing A one-paragraph essay

Should video websites warn teenagers about dangerous behavior?

A Read the essay and the Help note. Underline the topic sentence. Then add the words in the box to the sentences with supporting details. Use commas where necessary.

First	Second	Third	Finally

Video websites should warn teenagers about dangerous behavior for several reasons. Teenagers tend to take more risks because their brains are at a particular stage of development. With the rise in Internet video sites, teenagers can see people doing all kinds of dangerous activities, and some feel pressure to copy what they see. Some children are taking great risks and filming these activities so they can share the videos with their friends. The Internet makes sharing the videos easy – teens who want to impress their friends simply have to upload a clip to their profile page.

Help note: *Commas after listing expressions*
Use a comma after *First*, *Second*, *Third*, *Lastly*, and *Finally*.

B Editing Correct the errors in these sentences and add punctuation, where necessary. One sentence is correct.

I don't agree that video websites should have warnings for teenagers. At first many teenagers are very responsible. Second it is not the Internet's responsibility if someone does something dangerous. Third parents should be responsible for their children's behavior. At last the reasons for dangerous behavior are not always clear.

C Write a paragraph to answer the essay question. State your opinion in a clear topic sentence, and give at least three reasons to support it. Then check your paragraph for errors.

_____

_____

_____

_____

_____

_____

_____

_____

_____

Listening extra *Talk Tuesday*

A **What words and expressions would you expect to hear in a debate about television and children? Add four more ideas to the chart.**

get rid of TV   educational   a waste of time   fun

_____   _____   _____   _____

B ⬇️ **Listen to the introduction to a radio call-in show. Check (✔) the correct answers to the questions.**

1. What is the main topic of the show?
   ☐ a. Should children watch TV and if so, what type?
   ☐ b. Do children need a break from school work?
   ☐ c. Why do children spend too much time watching TV?

2. What are some of the topics that parents are debating?
   ☐ a. Should parents watch TV with their children?
   ☐ b. Should children watch TV at all?
   ☐ c. When should children watch TV?
   ☐ d. Should all children's TV programs be educational?

C ⬇️ **Listen to three callers to the radio show. Are the sentences true or false? Write T or F. Correct the false sentences.**

Mike   Michiko   Angelo

1. Mike is concerned about all the advertisements on TV that target kids. _____
2. He got rid of his TV a few years ago. _____
3. He believes children should spend their time in more useful ways. _____
4. Michiko thinks parents are the best teachers. _____
5. She thinks TV can be educational. _____
6. She's worried about her children watching shows in Spanish. _____
7. Angelo believes that watching TV is a big issue. _____
8. He thinks it's important that parents decide what children watch on TV. _____
9. He thinks the main problem is that people who watch TV are less intelligent. _____

About you

D ⬇️ **Listen again. Do you agree or disagree with the callers' opinions? Write one opinion that each caller gives, and complete the rest of the sentence with your own views.**

1. Mike says that _____ , which I think is _____ .
2. Michiko believes that _____ , and what's interesting is that _____ .
3. Angelo thinks that _____ , which is totally _____ .

Now complete the *Unit 2 Progress chart* on page 98.

Unit 2: The media   17

Lesson A Grammar Talking about the past

A Match the sentences with the correct timeline. Write a or b.

1. My English class has been so much more interesting since the winter break. __b__
2. When I was in high school, I studied in Mexico City for a semester. _____
3. I volunteered at a children's sports camp last summer. _____
4. Our teacher still hasn't given us our grades for the class project. _____
5. I've been taking violin lessons since elementary school. _____
6. My family moved to this neighborhood a few years ago. _____

a. past time   now

b. past time ⟶ now

B Circle the best verb forms to complete the sentences.

1. **Have you learned / Did you learn** Chinese when you were in Kunming?
2. So far, I **haven't traveled / didn't travel** to any other continents besides Europe.
3. After I **was getting / got** my license, I **have driven / drove** across the U.S. with my sister.
4. I **haven't been enjoying / didn't enjoy** my cooking class lately. I hope it gets better soon.
5. My brother **has joined / joined** a book club, but he **was quitting / quit** after a few weeks.
6. I really **have enjoyed / enjoyed** my job at the park last summer. I**'ve been working / was working** on the trails.

C Complete the conversations with the verbs given. Use an appropriate past tense or present perfect form. Sometimes more than one option may be possible.

1. *A* I haven't seen you in months! What have you been doing lately?
   B Oh, a lot of stuff, actually. I've been working (work) on my apartment – you know, cleaning and painting. I _____ (start) a few weekends ago, and it already looks great. How about you? What _____ (go on) with you lately?
   A Well, for the last month, I _____ (volunteer) as a tutor. I help kids with their homework after school. I _____ (be) surprised at first – it's actually a lot of fun. And there's my softball team, too. So far, I _____ (not score) any runs, but I never miss a game!

2. *A* Have you ever had a life-changing experience?
   B Actually, yeah. One semester, I _____ (work) at a homeless shelter. It _____ (not be) easy, you know, seeing people in such difficult situations, but I really _____ (love) the work. At the time, I _____ (major) in math, but after that semester I _____ (change) my major to social work, which I _____ (study) ever since. I _____ (not decide) what I want to do when I graduate, but I know I want to help people.

D Write true sentences about something . . .

1. you haven't done recently. I haven't gone bowling in a long time. I miss it!
2. you were doing earlier this year. _____
3. you've been doing regularly. _____
4. you did last weekend. _____
5. you haven't done yet (but need to soon!). _____

Lesson B Vocabulary Expressions for school

A Match the words in bold with the expressions that have a similar meaning. Write a–f.

a. fall behind on   c. miss   e. affect my grades
b. struggle with   d. complete the questions   f. leave it blank

1. It's a timed test. You have to **finish it** in 20 minutes. _____
2. I get really stressed-out when **I'm late with** my work. _____
3. When I get a cold, I usually **don't go to** a lot of classes. _____
4. I really **have a difficult time doing** math. It's been a problem since high school. _____
5. If I can't answer a question on an exam, I usually **don't write anything** at first, and then I come back to it later. _____
6. I've been going out too much, and it's really starting to **have a negative impact on my schoolwork**. _____

B Complete the conversation with the verbs in the box. Use each verb only once.

affect   count toward   ✔ finished   missed   turned . . . in
caught up on   fall behind on   left . . . blank   struggled with

A Have you ___finished___ your take-home exam yet?

B Yes, I _____ it _____ yesterday. It was tough – I really _____ it. What about you?

A I'm still having trouble. I've so much going on, and I'm starting to _____ my work.

B Yeah? Hey, what did you think about the second question?

A The second question? . . . Oh, right. Impossible. For now, I've just _____ it _____ .

B I know. I don't think I answered it very well. I know it'll _____ my grade.

A How much does this test _____ our final grade, anyway? Do you know?

B I have no idea. I _____ the first class when the professor explained all that stuff.

A Well, I sure will be glad when I've _____ my work. Then I'll be able to relax a little.

About you

C Answer the questions with information that is true for you.

1. What are two good reasons to miss a class?

_____

2. What can you do when you fall behind on your work?

_____

3. Do you think attendance should count toward your grade? Why or why not?

_____

4. When do you think it's better to leave a question blank on a test?

_____

5. What subjects or tasks do you sometimes struggle with?

_____

Lesson B Grammar Sequencing events

A **Which event happened first (1)? Which happened next (2)? Write 1 or 2 in each box.**

1. I was nervous the day of the exam ☐2☐, even though I'd been studying for over a week ☐1☐.
2. A classmate had warned me about this professor's tests ☐ , but I didn't believe him ☐ .
3. So later on, I asked my physics teacher for help ☐ . I'd managed to stop her in the hall ☐ .
4. I didn't do well on the exam ☐ , even though I'd asked that teacher for help ☐ .

B **Complete the conversations with the verbs given. Use the simple past, past perfect, or past perfect continuous. Sometimes there is more than one correct answer.**

1. *A* ___Had___ you ever ___lived___ (live) abroad before you _____ (move) here?

   B Yeah. One summer in grad school, I _____ (go) to Argentina and _____ (get) a job on a horse ranch.

   A Really? So have you been back to Argentina?

   B Yes! I _____ (go) back a few months ago. I _____ (think) about it for ages and finally _____ (decide) to go in August. I _____ (visit) my host family, who I _____ (not see) in years . . . and, of course, the horses!

2. *A* I haven't seen you in ages! What have you been up to?

   B Well, for one thing, I _____ (move) and _____ (change) jobs in April.

   A Wow, you left your cool publishing job? Why?

   B Well, things _____ (not go) well. I _____ (get) into an argument with my boss a few weeks before I _____ (quit), and things never really _____ (get) better.

3. *A* Why didn't you go to grad school?

   B Well, right before I _____ (graduate) from art school, I _____ (take) an entry-level job at a gallery. You know, I _____ (be) a little scared because I _____ (not earn) any money in a while. I _____ (hope) to go to grad school, but I _____ (need) money. So one day, I _____ (run) into a family friend that I _____ (not see) in a long time. When she found out I was an art major, she _____ (offer) me a job. And with the connections I've made, I'm actually selling some of my own paintings now!

C **Read the situations and complete the sentences with a correct form of the verbs given.**

1. I was waiting for my friends. An hour later, they finally showed up.
   When my friends finally _____ , I _____ for them for an hour. (show up / wait)

2. I called my advisor a few times last week. He never called back. I finally got an email from him yesterday.
   Yesterday I finally _____ an email from my advisor. I _____ him a few times last week, but he _____ . (get / call / not call back)

3. I cleaned my apartment last night. Then I did my homework. Then I watched TV.
   Last night I _____ my apartment, _____ my homework, and _____ TV. (clean / do / watch)

4. Last week our teacher reminded us to study the new vocabulary. On Monday he gave us a test. I was surprised.
   Our teacher _____ us a test on Monday. At first I was surprised, but then I remembered he _____ us to study last Friday. (give / remind)

Lesson C Conversation strategies

A Read the conversation. Circle the sentences when Jen interrupts her story, and underline the sentences when she comes back to it.

Jen Remember Mr. Jopling, our old history teacher? I ran into him yesterday.

Kim Really? Wow. Of course I remember him.

Jen Yeah, so I was in line right behind him. When I think about it, I just feel so ashamed. We were so awful to him.

Kim I know. It's embarrassing.

Jen So anyway, I saw him in line at the movies. He recognized me, and he even remembered my name. Twenty-five years later! Can you believe that? Looking back, I guess we probably made a pretty strong impression. We were constantly – I mean, constantly – passing notes back and forth. So yeah, where was I? Oh! So he told me he actually still has one of our notes.

Kim What? No way!

Jen Yeah. Get this. It's on his desk, in a frame. It says, in my handwriting, "I am sooooo bored." When I think about it, I just want to crawl under a rock. But anyway, you know what he told me? He told me that because of that note, he always tries hard to make his classes interesting.

Kim That's unbelievable. I mean, that's totally crazy.

B Match the sentences and the responses. Write the letters a–d.

1. When we were kids, my parents used to make us listen to opera every Sunday. _____

2. When I was little, I used to make clothes for all my dolls. _____

3. I love looking at old family pictures. _____

4. When I was a kid, I used to hang out in the kitchen as my grandmother prepared incredible meals. She was amazing! _____

a. Well, no wonder you hate it now!
b. No wonder you're such a good cook!
c. It's no wonder you became a fashion designer.
d. No wonder. They probably bring back great memories.

C Complete the anecdote with the expressions in the box. Write the letters a–e.

a. anyway   b. It's no wonder   c. Looking back   d. when I think about it   e. Where was I

"You know what I regret? I lost touch with my best friend from high school after we had a big fight. One day he told me about a personal problem and asked me not to tell anyone. I really wanted to help him, you know? But _____ , I was so young... I didn't know how to help. _____ ? Oh, right. So I asked another friend what she would do in my friend's situation. I didn't say his name, but she guessed who it was. _____ , I guess I thought I could trust her. I'll never make a mistake like that again, you know, telling someone else's secrets. So _____ , she told my best friend she knew about his problem. He was really embarrassed. _____ he hasn't spoken to me since."

Lesson D Reading A short story

A React Read the short story. Does it have a happy ending? Why or why not?

Lion

HOME

MENU

DISPLAY

BACK

1   When he was a small child, Lucas charged around the house like a lion. He roared, jumped out from behind the couch, slapped his tiny lion paws down on the table, and scared his baby sister. "Stop that!" his mother yelled, tugging his shirt hard. "You are not a lion. You are a little boy! Start acting like one!" Because he was not actually a lion, he thought maybe he could be a superhero. "But what do you really want to be?" his grandfather asked him one day as he slipped a dish of ice cream across the kitchen table. He wanted to be a police officer – or maybe a soldier or a firefighter. He wanted to be something big and strong, like a lion.

2   When Lucas was starting high school, his teachers said he was good at math. They said he should take advanced math classes. So he did, even though he didn't really like math. When he graduated from college, he told his father, "I want to travel. I want to see Africa." His father did not make eye contact. He said, "You're good at math. You could make a lot of money. Maybe you can be an engineer. Or do something in finance, say, be an investment banker."

3   So Lucas became an investment banker. He did not travel. He did not see Africa. He fell in love and was thinking about having a family. "I'll travel later," he thought. And so he was an investment banker, and he tried hard to enjoy it. He got married. His family grew. The years passed by. It was a good life, but he did not travel. He did not see Africa.

4   Soon Lucas wasn't an investment banker anymore, but a retired investment banker with nothing to do. To make matters worse, he was a retired investment banker who forgot

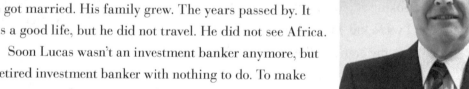

things. He forgot to turn off the oven, to bring in the mail, to take his medicine. Then he started forgetting more important things, like what his children did for a living and what his grandchildren's names were, and how many he had. He no longer acknowledged his neighbors – he had forgotten their names, too. And he forgot that he had once thought about venturing to Africa.

5   Then one afternoon when he had gone outside for a walk, Lucas looked up at the sky and forgot what his mother had told him. He forgot he was not a lion. He made his way toward a spot in the warm sun and lay down. He stretched out his big lion paws and felt a light breeze in his mane. He blinked his large lion eyes. A puffy white cloud was slowly making its way across the sky. He watched it until it had evaporated in the warm African air.

B **Check your understanding** Write the number of the paragraph next to each description.

1. Lucas is a middle-aged man who is struggling with his choices. _____
2. He is getting old, and it is having a negative effect on his memory. _____
3. He is young and carefree. _____
4. He must choose a career. _____
5. He is at the end of his life. _____

C **Read for main ideas** Choose the correct option to complete the sentences.

1. Lucas's mother yelled at him because she was _____ .
   a. having dinner   b. annoyed with him   c. scared of lions
2. Lucas's father didn't make eye contact because he wasn't _____ .
   a. happy with Lucas's plans   b. sure of his advice   c. interested in Lucas
3. In paragraph 3, we learn that Lucas _____ .
   a. didn't want to travel anymore   b. traveled for work   c. didn't like his job
4. In paragraph 4, we learn that Lucas _____ .
   a. was enjoying his retirement   b. had an illness   c. hated investment bankers
5. We learn in paragraph 5 that Lucas _____ .
   a. finally traveled to Africa   b. was very old   c. could no longer see

D **Focus on vocabulary** Replace the words and phrases in bold with words from the story.

slapped down
1. Lucas **put** his hands **down hard** on the table. (para. 1)

2. Lucas's mother pulled him away from his sister by **pulling on** his shirt. (para. 1)

3. Lucas's grandfather **moved** a dish of ice cream across the table. (para. 1)

4. When Lucas told his father he wanted to travel, his father didn't **look him in the eye**. (para. 2)

5. His father suggested he should be, **for example**, an engineer or an investment banker. (para. 2)

6. When Lucas got older and started forgetting things, he no longer **said hello to** his neighbors.

   (para. 4)

7. Lucas forgot that he had thought about **going somewhere risky, for example** to Africa. (para. 4)

8. He **walked** to a place in the sun and lay down. (para. 5)

E **React** Read the story again and answer the questions.

1. Which goals did Lucas achieve? Which goals did he not achieve?

   _____

   _____

2. Why do you think Lucas became an investment banker?

   _____

   _____

3. Why do you think Lucas never traveled to Africa?

   _____

   _____

Writing   A narrative article

A   Read the sentences in the box. Where do they belong in the narrative article below? Write the numbers 1–5.

> 1. I reached for my wallet and realized it was gone.
> 2. I was feeling a little tired and distracted.
> 3. I've often thought about that woman.
> 4. I live in a big city, so I'm pretty careful with my belongings.
> 5. She called my credit card company, which contacted me.

☐ I don't really lose things. But during the holidays last year, I was looking for gifts for my family at a large department store.

☐ After hours of searching, I found a few gifts and was standing in line to pay. ☐ I looked everywhere – I even went to the lost and found department – but my wallet was nowhere to be found.

I just started shaking. There had been about $500 in my wallet – my whole budget for the holidays! I finally gave up and left the store. About 15 minutes later, my phone rang.

A woman had found my wallet on a scarf display. ☐ She had seen all the cash and felt panicked for me. All the money was there when she returned my wallet, which is amazing. She said she'd never even thought about keeping the money. And even though I was really just thankful to have my wallet and all my credit cards back, I admit that I'd been worried about losing all that money.

☐ I guess that there are still honest people in this world – people who do the right thing.

B   Complete the narrative with appropriate forms of the verbs given.

It _____ (be) safe to assume that flights these days are going to be crowded. I usually _____ (prepare) myself for the worst. But the last time I traveled, I was amazed at how rude people were. I _____ (sit) quietly in my seat, and I _____ (read) a book. The man who _____ (sit) next to me _____ (hit) me with his elbow at least 20 times. Then the woman in front of me suddenly _____ (push) her seat back. She _____ (hurt) my knees and _____ (spill) my drink! The flight attendant _____ (bring) napkins, but I was totally soaked. Since then, I _____ always _____ (take) the train whenever possible!

C   Editing   Correct the mistakes in this narrative. There is one error in each sentence.

        spoken
I have always ~~spoke~~ to store clerks, but they don't always acknowledge me. One day I shop in a clothing store and needed help with a size. I have said, "Excuse me," but the salesperson ignored me. Finally, a manager was seeing me and asked if she could help. It was a good thing that someone finally helped me because I hadn't knew the sizes were for teenagers! Since then, I haven't went back to that store.

D   Write a narrative article for an online magazine about a time you experienced unexpected behavior from someone. Include an introduction, background events, main events, and a conclusion. Then check your article for errors.

Listening extra   Stories behind things

A   Think of a special possession, and write notes about it. Answer the questions.

- How did you get it? _____
- When did you get it? _____
- Does it remind you of (make you think of) anyone or anything? _____
- Is there a story behind it? _____

B   [⬇] Listen to Justin talk about items on his bookshelf. Check (✔) the three items he talks about.

☐   ☐   ☐   ☐   ☐

C   [⬇] Listen again and complete the chart.

	Justin's possession	How did he get it?	When did he get it?
1.			
2.			
3.			

D   [⬇] Listen again. Answer the questions.

1. Which item does Justin keep as a memory of . . .

   a. a person? _____

   b. a great time with friends? _____

   c. a life lesson? _____

2. Which item . . .

   a. does Justin use regularly? _____

   b. is not really his? _____

   c. did he get most recently? _____

E   Use your notes in Exercise A, and imagine you are telling a friend about your special possession. Write a short conversation.

_____

_____

_____

_____

Working lives

Lesson A Vocabulary Verb + noun collocations

A Match the two parts of each sentence. Write the letters a–f.

1. Employers like applicants who _____
2. Applicants should show that they are good at _____
3. Make sure you've done your homework on a company _____
4. If a candidate has training in a specialized area, _____
5. A résumé should highlight _____
6. If you have ideas about ways to save money for a company, _____

a. making progress and achieving goals on a project.
b. the résumé should clearly highlight it.
c. describe them in the interview.
d. show interest in the company and not just in the job itself.
e. before you submit an application.
f. the skills and knowledge a candidate has acquired in school or at another job.

B Complete the advice column from a career website. Use the correct form of the verbs in the box.

achieve	follow	make	show
face	have	meet	✔ submit

Promoting yourself in a
JOB INTERVIEW

HOME | LATEST NEWS | JOBS |

You have ___submitted___ an application, and the company has called you in for an interview. Now what? Here are a few tips to help you answer the tough questions and stand out from the crowd.

- "What are your strengths?" This is a popular question. Emphasize your ability to _____ deadlines, _____ the company money, and beat the competition with creative ideas. Give examples.

- "What are your weaknesses?" Always answer this in a positive way. Give an example of a weakness, explain how you deal with it, and show your willingness to _____ advice.

- "Why should we hire you?" This is an opportunity to highlight any training you _____ . It is also important to describe how you can collaborate with others to _____ goals.

- "Do you have any questions?" Always have at least one question ready to ask the interviewer. Make sure you have done your homework before the interview, and ask intelligent questions about the company and the job. You are probably _____ stiff competition, and this _____ your interest in the company.

At the end of the interview, thank the interviewer and ask for a business card. Don't forget to follow up a few days later with a thank-you email.

Lesson A Grammar Types of nouns

A Complete the conversation with a correct form of the nouns given. Add *a/an* or make the noun plural, where necessary.

Macy Hey, Jack, could you help me with something, please? I need _____ (advice)!

Jack Sure. What's up?

Macy Well, I'm putting together _____ (application) for a job as a personal assistant, and I need _____ (feedback) on my résumé. I wonder if you could give me some _____ (comment).

Jack OK, let me see. Well, you've got _____ (information) here about your last job at the clothing store, but there's not much here about the _____ (training) you've had as a receptionist. I think that's more important.

Macy Yeah, I guess that *is* _____ (detail) I could add. Receptionists and personal assistants do similar _____ (job). I mean, they do similar types of _____ (work).

Jack Have you talked to anyone who is _____ (personal assistant)? In the interview, you'll need to show that you have some _____ (knowledge) of the job.

Macy Yeah, I got _____ (help) from _____ (counselor) at an agency. She was really nice.

Jack Great. Well, it sounds like you're all set, then.

B Complete the sentences with the correct simple present form of the verbs.

1. Today, more and more highly qualified candidates _____ for low-level jobs. (apply)
2. A lot of work experience _____ always necessary to land your dream job. (not be)
3. The research you do _____ an employer that you're interested in the company. (show)
4. Be sure all the relevant information about your jobs _____ on your résumé. (appear)
5. A lot of graduates from my school _____ careers in education. (choose)
6. Specialized knowledge _____ often necessary for jobs in science and engineering. (be)

About you

C Complete the questions with a correct form of the nouns and verbs given. Then answer the questions with information that is true for you.

1. What personal _____ (information) _____ (be) appropriate on a résumé?

   _____

2. Who have you asked for help with your résumé? What _____ (feedback) _____ (be) the most helpful?

   _____

3. What _____ (be) some of your most important career _____ (goal)?

   _____

4. What special _____ (knowledge) _____ (be) necessary to do your dream job?

   _____

5. What _____ (training) _____ (be) required for careers you're interested in? Or _____ (be) there any special _____ (training)?

   _____

Lesson B Grammar Generalizing and specifying

A Look at each noun or noun phrase in bold. Is the speaker making a generalization (G) or talking about a specific person or thing (S)? Write G or S.

1. "Could you please send **the feedback** on my résumé to my personal email address?" _____

2. "Sometimes **advice** that contradicts your own ideas is hard to take." _____

3. "I always take my gym clothes to **the office**." _____

4. "I would just really love a health club right in **the building**." _____

5. "When I find **a company** that offers **good health insurance**, I'll be happy." _____ _____

6. "**The advice** you gave me was invaluable." _____

B Complete the blog post with *a/an*, *the*, or – (no article).

| BLOG | PODCASTS 🎧 | PROGRAMS | LISTEN LIVE |

So, most of you know I'm looking for _____ job. And most of you know that I haven't had much luck so far! Well, I've decided to write _____ description of my dream company, just in case anyone is reading! :-) My dream company has _____ office with _____ window for each employee. It offers _____ good benefits, like _____ health insurance. In the building, there are _____ great perks – like _____ gym with _____ sauna, and _____ room where employees can lie down and take _____ nap. _____ Spanish classes at lunchtime are free, and you can take _____ other classes after work. This company lets you listen to _____ music in _____ office, but you shouldn't disturb others. And it's family friendly: It offers _____ child care, and if _____ kids want to come hang out with you at lunch, that's OK, too.

So what do you think? What's your dream company like? What are _____ perks and benefits that you'd like?

posted Sunday, July 24 at 8:13 p.m.

About you

C Answer the questions with information that is true for you.

1. What is more important to you, a high salary or a lot of vacation time? Why?

   _____

   _____

2. Do you like to listen to music at work, or do you prefer peace and quiet? Why?

   _____

   _____

3. Would you rather have paid overtime or flexible work hours? Why?

   _____

   _____

Lesson C Conversation strategies

A Complete the conversation with the adverbs in the box. Use each adverb only once.

clearly	interestingly enough	seriously	unfortunately

Chris Do you think I'll ever find a job?

Mara Oh, Chris! Are you kidding?

Chris _____ , I'm getting discouraged.

Mara Don't worry. Something will come up. You're working hard, _____ . I mean, you're sending out résumés every day!

Chris Well, I'm emailing résumés to companies that haven't actually advertised job openings. You know, companies I researched and would like to work for. I just don't know if I'm making any progress.

Mara Yeah, but you never know. _____ , I just saw something about this on a career website. It said employers like candidates who've done their homework on the company.

Chris I guess so. I would just love some positive feedback.

Mara Well, _____ , it just might take some time.

B Circle the appropriate response to complete each conversation.

1. *A* Do you ever feel stuck in your job? I mean, do you wish you could do something else?
   B Well, not really. In fact, **I'm looking for something right now / I really love my career choice.**

2. *A* Does your company offer subsidized transportation to and from work?
   B Yeah, and as a matter of fact, **I need to use it more often / they offer discounted transportation**!

3. *A* How's your job search going? Have you found anything?
   B I've had several offers but not the right one yet. In fact, **I rejected an offer today / I haven't found a job**.

4. *A* Is it difficult to find work these days?
   B Actually, no. In fact, they say **there are more jobs than ever / there's really high unemployment**.

C Complete the conversation. Write the letters a–e.

Alma I'm thinking about changing careers. I don't make enough money teaching economics. _____

Felipe Yeah, but your job is so "you." _____

Alma Yeah, luckily, I do love teaching. _____

Felipe You could ask for a raise. _____

Alma I can't really do that. But I could do some tutoring, I guess. _____

a. Seriously, you can't tell me you'd leave teaching just to get a better salary.
b. In fact, I think I'll start looking into it.
c. But unfortunately, with my salary, I just can't save any money.
d. Clearly, I should get a job at a bank or something.
e. Oddly enough, sometimes all you have to do is ask.

Lesson D Reading Job offers

A Prepare How important to you are the factors below when you are evaluating a job offer? Give each factor a number from 0 (not at all important) to 10 (extremely important).

- ☐ the cafeteria
- ☐ company culture
- ☐ opportunities for training
- ☐ opportunities to travel on business
- ☐ opportunity to work from home
- ☐ where the company is
- ☐ your boss's personality
- ☐ your personal wants and needs

B Read for main ideas Read the post from a career website. Which of the factors in Exercise A are mentioned?

IS THIS JOB RIGHT FOR ME?
Evaluating a job offer

1 So, you've just been offered a job. The long, difficult search is over, right? Well, maybe not. As a matter of fact, you haven't faced the real challenge yet. When you get a job offer, it's hard not to get excited and just accept it. But don't let your excitement make you forget about the importance of this decision.

Of course you'll think about salary and benefits as you evaluate a job offer. But how do you decide if a particular job is right for you? Interestingly enough, salary and benefits might not be the most important factors to consider. Here are some things to think about as you make your assessment.

2 ▶ ☐ Obviously, you're going to think about yourself when you make your decision. But be careful not to make a decision based on someone else's opinion. For example, don't take a job because your parents or friends think you should. This is the time to put a high value on your own wants and needs. You will be the one who has to go to work and do the job every day.

3 ▶ ☐ What is this company really like? Do employees seem to like one another and collaborate well together? Clearly, this is hard to see if you don't already work for the company, but you can assess some things in very little time. How did you feel during your interviews at the company? Do people seem happy? Are their workspaces bright and welcoming? Did you notice anything that made you uncomfortable? If a voice in your head is warning you about the company culture, it's a good idea to listen to that voice.

4 ▶ ☐ Does the job honestly seem interesting to you? Will it challenge you? Will there be a need for some of the skills and training you have from previous jobs or internships? You'll be spending more than 2,000 hours a year at work. Certainly you want that time to be challenging and rewarding.

5 ▶ ☐ Will you have a chance to acquire skills and knowledge you don't already have? Are there opportunities for you to get new training? Most importantly, is there a good chance that you'll get promotions and work your way up in the company over time? You'll want to think about long-term as well as short-term career growth.

6 ▶ ☐ Your boss can make your job a wonderful experience or a terrible one. Will you be able to learn from this person? Will he or she offer guidance and give constructive criticism, and help find a solution whenever difficult problems pop up? If so, this may be the right fit for you. However, if you feel that you and your boss won't get along, this can have a negative effect on your performance, and unfortunately, you might have to look elsewhere.

7 ▶ ☐ Your potential new job is in a busy city (but you feel overwhelmed by large cities), and your daily commute will be long (and possibly crowded). Or the company is located too far from a city center (and there are no shops or cafés around). If either of these is true, is it OK with you?

There are many factors you need to consider when assessing a job offer. It's also a good idea to get some specialized advice and guidance from a career counselor or a professional you know. If you examine these factors, along with salary and benefits, you are on your way to making the best decision you can.

C **Information flow** **Where do these headings fit in the article? Write the letters a–f in the boxes in the article.**

    a. Company culture

    b. Location

    c. Opportunities for growth

    d. The position

    e. Your new boss

    f. Yourself

D **Focus on vocabulary** **Complete the nouns in bold with the correct endings. Use the article on page 30 to help you.**

1. You should consider the **imp**_____ of training and opportunities to learn new things. (para. 1) ❑

2. One way to make an **assess**_____ of a company's culture is to look around at people's workspaces. (para. 1) ❑

3. If you put a high **val**_____ on your free time, you should ask about vacations and days off. (para. 2) ❑

4. If you have a **ne**_____ for specialized advice, you should see a career counselor. (para. 4) ❑

5. You should take a lot of **gui**_____ from other people before you accept any job. (para. 6) ❑

6. Getting constructive **critic**_____ from a boss will have a negative effect on your performance. (para. 6) ❑

7. According to the article, the **sol**_____ to the problem of finding the right job is straightforward. (para. 6) ❑

E **Read for main ideas** **Decide if the sentences in Exercise D are true, false, or if the information is not given in the article. Write T, F, or NG in the boxes above.**

About you

F **React** **Answer the questions with information that is true for you.**

1. In your opinion, what are the two most important reasons for rejecting a job offer?

    _____

    _____

2. What do you think are the two most important things to look for in a company's culture?

    _____

    _____

3. Why do you think it's important to acquire new skills at work?

    _____

    _____

4. Is company location important to you? Why or why not?

    _____

    _____

5. Who do you go to for advice when making important decisions? Why?

    _____

    _____

Writing A personal statement

A Read the excerpt from a personal statement on a job application. In what order do these topics appear? Number the topics 1–5.

introduction ____	studies ____	work experience ____
leisure time ____	summary ____	

I have been interested in international relations since I took an economics class in my junior year of high school. I started an exchange program at my school, and during my senior year, I organized an exchange with a group of students from Mexico City. **I decided** to study international relations in college because **I was interested** in a wide range of subjects, including global economics, political science, international law, and finance. Last summer, I had an internship at an international law firm. **I was responsible for** attending client meetings and writing reports. My manager **guided** me, and I received training in planning and making assessments. In my free time, I volunteer at an immigrant center. This work has been invaluable because I have met people from all over the world and helped them **solve** their various problems. I am ready to use my skills and knowledge in a challenging work environment. I feel my education and experience have prepared me for a position with an international company.

B Rewrite these sentences from Exercise A with the noun forms of the words in bold.

1. ___My interest___ in international relations began when I took an economics class in my junior year of high school.

2. _____ to study international relations in college was based on _____ in a wide range of subjects . . .

3. _____ included attending client meetings and writing reports.

4. I received _____ from my manager.

5. I have met people from all over the world and helped them find _____ to their various problems.

C Editing Correct the sentences. There is one error in each sentence.

1. During my internship, I learned how to use all the latest softwares that designers use today.

2. Last summer, I received a training in new information systems.

3. I received constructive advices from my manager, which helped me improve my skills.

4. I am looking for a work in a technology company.

5. I gained an experience in solving clients problems.

D Write a personal statement for a job application. Then check your personal statement for errors.

My interest in architecture began in high school and was encouraged by my art teacher . . .

Listening extra A career expert

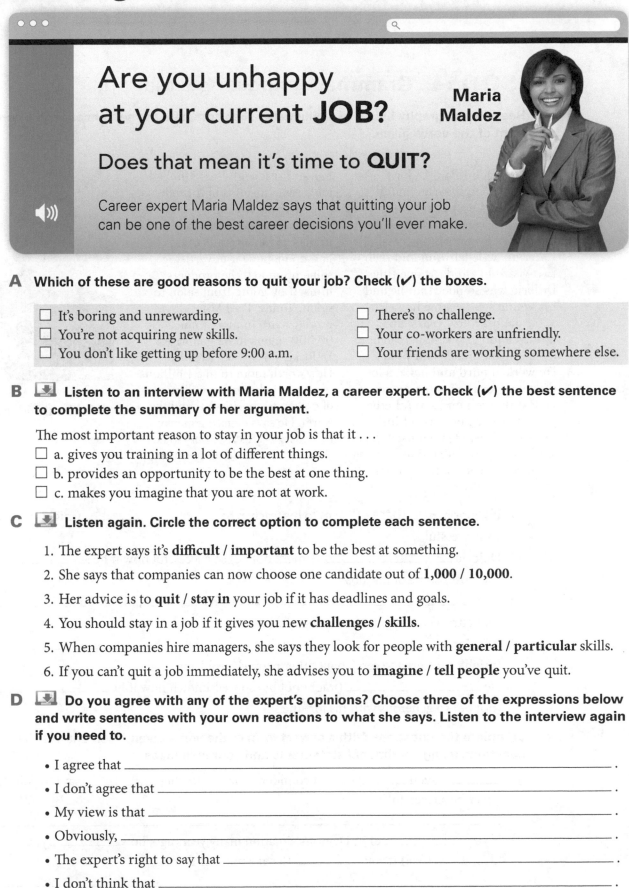

Are you unhappy at your current JOB?

Maria Maldez

Does that mean it's time to QUIT?

Career expert Maria Maldez says that quitting your job can be one of the best career decisions you'll ever make.

A **Which of these are good reasons to quit your job? Check (✔) the boxes.**

☐ It's boring and unrewarding.
☐ You're not acquiring new skills.
☐ You don't like getting up before 9:00 a.m.

☐ There's no challenge.
☐ Your co-workers are unfriendly.
☐ Your friends are working somewhere else.

B **Listen to an interview with Maria Maldez, a career expert. Check (✔) the best sentence to complete the summary of her argument.**

The most important reason to stay in your job is that it . . .
☐ a. gives you training in a lot of different things.
☐ b. provides an opportunity to be the best at one thing.
☐ c. makes you imagine that you are not at work.

C **Listen again. Circle the correct option to complete each sentence.**

1. The expert says it's **difficult / important** to be the best at something.

2. She says that companies can now choose one candidate out of **1,000 / 10,000**.

3. Her advice is to **quit / stay in** your job if it has deadlines and goals.

4. You should stay in a job if it gives you new **challenges / skills**.

5. When companies hire managers, she says they look for people with **general / particular** skills.

6. If you can't quit a job immediately, she advises you to **imagine / tell people** you've quit.

D **Do you agree with any of the expert's opinions? Choose three of the expressions below and write sentences with your own reactions to what she says. Listen to the interview again if you need to.**

- I agree that _____ .
- I don't agree that _____ .
- My view is that _____ .
- Obviously, _____ .
- The expert's right to say that _____ .
- I don't think that _____ .

Now complete the *Unit 4 Progress chart* on page 99.

Unit 4: Working lives

5

Challenges

Lesson A Grammar Imagining situations

A **Read the biography below of a billionaire. Then complete the sentences with a correct form of the verbs given.**

When John Paul DeJoria was in high school, his classmates voted him "Least Likely to Succeed." Even a teacher told him, "You'll never be successful." Later his wife left him and their two-year-old child. At one time, DeJoria was so poor that he and his young son became homeless.

Luckily, a few years later, he landed a job as a salesperson at a company that made hair products. He worked hard and made a lot of money for the company, but he lost that job and several other jobs afterward because of his unusual ideas. He then used the skills and knowledge that he had acquired to collaborate with a hairstylist friend, Paul Mitchell, and create his own hair products.

After borrowing $700 to start the business, DeJoria lived in his car for several weeks. He had no money for advertising, so he promoted the products himself by going from salon to salon. Today, Paul Mitchell products are in more than 90,000 salons in 82 countries. DeJoria is now very wealthy: He's worth more than $4 billion.

DeJoria has given millions of dollars to charities around the world. He says donating money to charity is effective, but "so is showing up and doing something."

John Paul DeJoria

1. If DeJoria _had listened_ (listen) to his teacher, he _____ (might not become) so successful.

2. DeJoria _____ (might not be) so successful now if he _____ (not lose) some of his jobs.

3. If he _____ (not collaborate) with a hairstylist, his products _____ (not attract) the attention of so many salons.

4. If DeJoria _____ (not become) homeless, he _____ (might not learn) to care about other people's problems.

5. He _____ (might not be) so well-known now if he _____ (not be) so generous with his fortune.

About you

B **Complete the questions with a correct form of the verbs given. Then answer the questions using conditional statements and your own ideas.**

1. _____ you _____ (be) confident now if a teacher _____ (say) to you, "You'll never be successful"?

_____

2. If you _____ (be) in DeJoria's situation many years ago, how _____ you _____ (feel) if you _____ (lose) a number of jobs?

_____

Lesson B Vocabulary Problems and solutions

Complete the conversations with the words in the boxes.

create	creation	investment	invests	poor	✔ poverty	wealth	wealthy

1. **A** Look at that homeless woman with her children. It's so depressing. ___Poverty___ is such a huge problem in this city. So many _____ families are struggling.

 B I know. The distribution of _____ is a real issue. I can't believe how incredibly _____ some people are. Seriously, what do they *do* with all that money?

 A I know what you mean. Clearly, the government _____ in job _____ , but it seems that the jobs they _____ are either low paying or highly specialized.

 B Yeah, I wish there were more _____ in education and job training. Then more people would have a chance.

eradicate	eradication	invest	investment	starvation	starving

2. **A** Do you know anything about investing? We've been thinking we want to _____ in companies that give back to the community in some way.

 B You mean that do charitable work? Or companies that make vaccines or something to _____ childhood diseases? I know some companies that are working towards the _____ of malaria.

 A Yeah. That or companies that help people who are _____ , for example.

 B Right. _____ is a huge problem. Well, hmm, you probably should check it out online. But it's a great idea – making an _____ in socially responsible companies can make a big difference.

distributing	distribution	hunger	hungry	unemployed	unemployment

3. **A** What did you do this weekend?

 B Oh, the usual. On Sunday I worked at the food bank _____ food.

 A Really? I didn't know you were doing volunteer work.

 B Yeah. You know, I can't just do nothing when people are _____ . Our food bank is responsible for the _____ of more than 5,000 meals a week, which is a lot for a small town.

 A Wow! I didn't realize that _____ was such a problem here.

 B It's pretty serious. And with very high _____ rates, the situation isn't getting any better. Fortunately, though, not all the people who come to us are homeless. Many have homes, but are _____ , you know, they're struggling to find a job.

eradication	pollution	protect	protection

4. **A** I'm so tired of reading about large corporations polluting the environment.

 B I know. I just can't understand why _____ is still a problem in this day and age! I mean, don't people realize we all have to _____ the environment? Why don't governments pass stricter environmental _____ laws? That should be easy.

 A Well, not really. It's expensive to do things the "green" way.

 B But if greener methods lead to the total _____ of pollution, we all win.

Lesson B Grammar Wishes, hopes, and regrets

A **Circle the correct form of the verbs to complete the sentences.**

1. I'd forgotten that my friend's husband had lost his job. I really wish I **hadn't brought up** / **didn't bring up** the unemployment issue when we were having lunch last week.

2. The distribution of wealth is so imbalanced in this country. I hope the government **would do** / **will do** something about it in the near future.

3. I wish more people **would stop** / **stop** buying bottled water. It would go a long way toward protecting the environment.

4. I hope this year's political debates **include** / **would include** the pollution issue. We have so many polluted rivers in our area!

5. I wish the government **could** / **will** eradicate poverty in our country.

6. My responsibilities at work include buying gifts for clients. I wish I **will have signed up** / **had signed up** for the green committee instead.

B **Read the conversations. Complete the responses with a correct form of the verbs given. Sometimes more than one answer is possible.**

1. *A* You know, the government doesn't do enough to protect the environment.
   B You're absolutely right. I wish environmental protection _____ (be) a top priority.

2. *A* There are so many hungry children in our country. It's very sad.
   B I know. I wish the government _____ (spend) more to eradicate hunger. It's just not a priority for them right now.

3. *A* Did you hear about the most recent unemployment numbers? The rate is the lowest in history.
   B That's great news! I just wish it _____ (get) that low last year when a lot of my friends were looking for jobs.

4. *A* Do you think they'll ever find a solution to the city's traffic problems?
   B Who knows? But I hope they _____ (invest) in some new buses. The old ones are always breaking down.

About you

C **Complete the sentences with your own ideas.**

1. Water pollution is a huge problem all over the world. (I hope . . .)
   I hope governments will work together to clean up our polluted rivers and oceans.
   _____

2. Starvation is such a huge problem in the poorest countries. (I hope . . .)
   _____

3. There's a shortage of housing. They just haven't built enough homes. (I wish . . .)
   _____

4. There are not enough good jobs for people. (I wish . . .)
   _____

Lesson C Conversation strategies

A Complete the conversation with the expressions in the box. Use each expression at least once. Sometimes more than one answer is possible.

imagine	suppose	what if

Anne A friend of mine is having a surprise party for her husband. Instead of gifts, she's asking people to bring books to donate to the local library. Cool, huh?

Raj _____ people don't have any used books that are in good condition?

Anne Well, _____ you were invited to the party. What would you do?

Raj You know me: I have tons of books at home, so it wouldn't be a problem.

Anne I guess most people would rather buy books than other things – like clothes and stuff. _____ someone threw a party for you and asked people to do something for a charity? Would you be upset if you didn't get gifts?

Raj Me? No way. I really don't need a thing.

B Check (✔) the appropriate response in each conversation.

1. *A* The problem for me with holidays is all the gifts you have to buy. It's just so expensive.
    B ❑ I suppose. It doesn't cost very much, though.
        ❑ I suppose it is. Though I just set a budget and stick to it.

2. *A* Would you ever return a gift and get the money instead?
    B ❑ I don't think so. I suppose it wouldn't seem right.
        ❑ Yeah, I suppose I would. It's nice to keep the gift.

3. *A* I like to buy gifts in local stores. It's nice to support small neighborhood businesses.
    B ❑ That's true. I suppose it's better to go to a large shopping mall or something.
        ❑ I suppose it is. You can get unusual things, too. The big stores all have the same stuff.

C Complete the conversation with *suppose, imagine, I suppose, I imagine,* and *what if . . . ?* Sometimes more than one answer is possible.

A I don't know what to do with all these toys. They're in great condition, but the kids don't play with them anymore.

B Well, _____ we donated them to that homeless shelter downtown?

A Actually, that's a great idea. I mean, _____ you were a homeless child: even one toy would make you happy, _____ .

B Yeah, I just wish more people would think about the homeless situation in our city. People have too much, and they give too little. _____ everyone gave just one used toy or a book or even an old coat?

A And if people gave more, _____ the shelter would be so much more comfortable.

B Which is why we should go take these toys down to the shelter right now.

A Yeah. Let's do it.

Lesson D Reading Medical charities

A Prepare What problems do you think international medical charities help with? Check (✔) the boxes below.

☐ building homes for the homeless   ☐ finding jobs for the unemployed
☐ cleaning up rivers and lakes   ☐ preventing disease
☐ clearing up after natural disasters   ☐ treating illnesses

B Read for main ideas Read the article. Which of the issues in Exercise A are mentioned in the article?

The work of an international medical charity

1 Every year thousands of international volunteers – doctors, surgeons, nurses, dentists, clean water experts, and other professionals – are sent by medical charities to help local medical workers. Here we talk to a few volunteers about their experiences.

2 *LINDA JONES, a nurse, was one of hundreds of volunteers who flew to a devastated area after an enormous earthquake.*

3 *Q* **Do people usually come together during a disaster?**
A The devastation after the earthquake was just huge. Large parts of the region were completely destroyed, but the community really did come together. I suppose it might be surprising, but in my experience most people help each other during natural disasters. As we were clearing up we found a woman, for example, who was looking after a neighbor's five-month-old baby and her two-year-old sister. Their mother was too sick to take care of them, and their father was devastated. But he also had to work. . . . If the neighbor hadn't helped, the father wouldn't have been able to work, and he might have lost his job. There are lots of stories like this. I don't know what we would have done if we hadn't had this kind of help with the sick and injured from the community.

4 *Another volunteer, **TIM MENDES**, a general surgeon, helped to remove injured patients from a war zone.*

5 *Q* **How do you safely remove the injured from war zones?**
A It always depends. Recently I worked with a team to get people out of a dangerous area by boat. There was a large number of patients, so our idea was that it would be quicker to get them out by a floating ambulance. Many had life-threatening injuries. We had several doctors and nurses, and even one dentist who had some emergency medical training. Everyone was helping.

6 It was a difficult journey. Everyone was seasick. We had to take care of people, but we couldn't even stand up! The boat trip was 10 long hours, but it was amazing when we landed safely and there were 18 ambulances waiting to take the patients to the hospital.

7 Despite the bad weather and the rough conditions on the boat, it was a successful operation. If we hadn't used a boat, a lot of people wouldn't have been saved.

8 *DR. MARGARET WINTERS is a project coordinator at a large international medical charity.*

9 *Q* **What happens when there isn't enough money or resources to treat illnesses?**
A It's a real problem and I wish there were an easy solution because millions of people continue to suffer and die from common diseases that could be prevented. In a lot of the countries that we work in, we see people with lumps and growths that become enormous. This simply wouldn't happen in wealthier countries. Often they're not malignant, you know they're benign tumors, but without treatment they cause a lot of suffering for the people concerned. We're always hoping that governments will invest more in our work.

C Read for main ideas **Read the article again. Who talks about . . .**

1. health care in poor countries? _____
2. patients with serious injuries? _____
3. a family? _____
4. a floating ambulance? _____
5. the need for more resources? _____

D Focus on vocabulary **Choose the word that best completes each sentence.**

benign	devastation	injured	treatment
dentists	enormous	sick	tumor
devastated	huge	surgeons	

1. International volunteers include many medical professionals such as doctors, _____ , nurses, and _____ .
2. After a _____ earthquake, doctors flew to the regions that were most affected by the _____ .
3. People often come together after a natural disaster even though they all feel _____ by what has happened.
4. It's important that doctors are able to help the _____ and _____ as soon as possible.
5. It can be an _____ problem to remove sick people from war zones.
6. A small lump can quickly turn into a large growth or _____ . Sometimes it's _____ and not harmful or malignant, but it's still a problem.
7. In richer countries, patients receive _____ for common health problems earlier.

E Read for detail **Are the sentences true or false? Write T or F. Correct the false sentences.**

1. Linda Jones was not surprised that people came together after the earthquake. _____

2. The neighbor helped the father find a job. _____

3. The dentist only helped people who had problems with their teeth. _____

4. They used 18 floating ambulances to remove people from the war zone. _____

5. There is not an easy solution to finding money and resources to treat illnesses. _____

6. In richer countries people have the same health problems as in poorer ones. _____

F React **Answer the questions about the article. Give your own views.**

1. What do you think about these volunteers and the work they do?
_____
_____

2. Whose job was the most difficult do you think? Why?
_____
_____

3. If you were able to volunteer, what kinds of work would you prefer to do?
_____
_____

Writing An inquiry

A **Read the email inquiry. Add *it* where necessary in the underlined parts of the sentences.**

Dear Mr. Thomas:

I'm interested in volunteering at the national park this summer. I've hiked and camped in the park all my life, and <u>I would love to do trail maintenance</u> and help pick up trash.

On your website, <u>says that park volunteers live in tents</u> in the park. I live a few miles away, and I <u>would prefer if</u> I could go home at the end of the day. <u>Would be a problem if</u> I went home at night and came back to the park in the morning?

In addition, <u>would be very nice if</u> I could bring my dog. I couldn't find anything on the website about this. <u>Is possible to</u> bring pets into the park?

I <u>would appreciate if</u> you could send me more details about the volunteer program and the application form for volunteers. <u>Thank you for your attention.</u> <u>I look forward to hearing from you.</u>

Sincerely, Carlos Almieva

B **Unscramble the sentences.**

1. if / could / a current volunteer / It / useful / would be / I / speak to

   _____ .

2. if / begin working / I / love / immediately / could / would / it / I

   _____ .

3. if / a problem / it / when I arrive / Would / paid / I / be

   _____ ?

4. more information / it / you / I / send me / appreciate / would / if / could

   _____ .

C **Editing** **Correct these sentences. There is one error in each one.**

1. Will be interesting to read about your training program.

2. Would be a problem for me if I had to wait another week to start?

3. Is difficult for me to commute on the bus.

4. Would be useful if I could arrive a day early?

5. Was interesting to read your website.

D **Write an email inquiry to a volunteer program. Use an idea in the box or your own idea. Then check your email for errors.**

| read books to children at a literacy center | volunteer at a city park |
| teach a craft at a homeless shelter | volunteer at a home for the elderly |

Listening extra Making a difference

A Rewrite the sentences by replacing the words in bold with the words in the box.
Then answer the questions with your own ideas.

charitable organization	connected	donors	requests	support

1. Would you like to **give money to** a charity more often?

   Q: _____

   A: _____

2. What's the name of your favorite **charity**?

   Q: _____

   A: _____

3. How do charities stay **in touch** with **the people who give money**?

   Q: _____

   A: _____

4. How often do you get **letters that ask** for donations?

   Q: _____

   A: _____

B 📥 Listen to an extract from a TV show. Check (✔) the
sentences that give the speaker's views.

☐ She wishes people would stop supporting some charities.
☐ She thinks the only way to help a charity is to give money.
☐ She thinks local charities often find it hard to raise money.
☐ She hopes she'll be able to do more projects in the future.

C 📥 Listen again. Complete the sentences with no more than three words.

1. Sunny has always felt strongly about world issues like poverty and the _____ .

2. People tend to stop giving to charity because they don't know what happens to _____ .

3. Small charities who are looking for money for projects can _____ on Sunny's website.

4. People who give small amounts of money still like to feel that they are _____ .

5. Some donors like to give to college students who are _____ .

6. A new kindergarten just received $1000 for _____ .

About you

D Answer the questions with your own ideas and opinions.

1. What do you think about Sunny's idea?

   _____

2. Is it better to support international charities or ones in your own area? Why?

   _____

3. What are some other ways charities can stay connected with the people who support them?

   _____

Now complete the *Unit 5 Progress chart* on page 99.

Into the future

Lesson A Grammar Describing future events

A Use the words given to write sentences about future events.

1. We / will / be / live / in a totally cashless society by 2050.
   <u>We'll be living in a totally cashless society by 2050.</u>

2. People / won't / be / use / credit or debit cards.

   _____

3. Everybody / be going to / be / do / their banking online.

   _____

4. People / won't / be / write / checks anymore.

   _____

5. We / be going to / be / carry / around fewer gadgets generally.

   _____

6. Everyone / will / be / do / all their grocery shopping on the Internet.

   _____

B Circle the correct option to complete the conversation.

A Hey, did I tell you? My boss said I'm going to get a new tablet for work!

B Lucky you! What **are you using / are you going to use** it for?

A Well, **I'll take / I take** it with me if **I'll visit / I visit** clients. But I guess when **I need / I'll need** to do a lot of typing, **I still use / I'll still use** my laptop.

B So, do you think tablets **replace / will replace** laptops in the future?

A Well, I don't think laptops **are going to disappear / disappear**, but they probably **won't be / aren't** as popular in the future.

B I suppose we **might use / use** them less if tablets **will become / become** more common.

A Yeah. I suppose that's inevitable.

About you

C Answer the questions with your own ideas.

1. What device(s) do you think you'll be using for work and for fun in five years from now?

   _____

2. Do you think one device will ever replace all the devices people use now? Why or why not?

   _____

3. Design your dream device. What will it be able to do?

   _____

Lesson B Vocabulary Expressions used in presentations

A Read the beginning of a presentation. Write the letter of each expression a–h in the appropriate place.

Good morning. I'm Liu Peng, director of the Global Conference on the Future of Technology. Thank you for coming. Today's speaker is an expert in the field of transportation engineering. Her designs have won awards in cities all over the world. So ☐ to her now. Everyone, please welcome Helena Lopes.

Thank you, Liu Peng. Good morning, everyone. Um, ☐ in the back? OK, great. Oh, and did you all pick up a handout by the door on your way in? If you don't have one, raise your hand because ☐ now. Everybody has one? Great.

Today, as part of our series on the future of technology, ☐ the future of transportation, and in particular, trains. ☐ my talk by taking a general look at transportation issues in both urban and rural areas, and talk about possible solutions. After that, ☐ and look at new developments in transportation technology. Please save your questions for later, as ☐ . There's a lot of information to present, and I want to get through it all. So ☐ . (. . .)

GLOBAL CONFERENCE ON THE FUTURE OF TECHNOLOGY

Rio de Janeiro, Brazil
MAY 21–25

Helena Lopes

a. I want to look at
b. I'd like to begin
c. I'll allow time at the end
d. can everybody hear me

e. let's get started
f. we'll move on
g. they should be going around
h. I'll turn it over

B Complete the end of the presentation with the words in the box.

comments	questions	stop
handout	saying	time

(. . .) So, as you'll see on page 10 of the _____ , there are many new technologies that promise to help solve tomorrow's transportation problems. And as I have shown today, trains will be contributing in large part to those solutions.

Well, since it's almost 3:00, I'd better _____ there, because that's all I have _____ for today. I'll just conclude by _____ that you're going to be seeing a lot of exciting new changes in train transportation in the future. So, um, does anyone have any _____ or _____ ?

Lesson B Grammar Modal verbs

A Complete what the presenter says. Match each sentence with the most logical second sentence. Write the letters a–d.

1. Does everyone have a handout? _____
2. So, let's move on and watch a short clip. _____
3. OK, we're running out of time. _____
4. We have to stop now. _____

a. I'd better stop here and answer your questions.
b. Thank you for coming.
c. Everyone should have one by now.
d. Could somebody turn the lights off, please?

B Circle the best option to complete the extracts from a presentation.

1. **Can / Would** everyone hear me? If not, I **might want to / could** turn up the sound.
2. The sound's not on? The microphone **must / had better** be turned off. **Would / Must** someone check it for me? Thanks.
3. Now, everyone **might want to / ought to** have a handout by now. If you didn't get one, you **might want to / would** share with the person next to you.
4. So, **would / can** I ask a question? How many of you **had better / can** pay all your bills online?
5. Well, it's 11:30, so we**'d better / would** stop here. The next group **might / won't** be waiting for the room. Thank you for coming.

C Use the modal verbs in the boxes to rewrite the underlined parts of the presentations.

✔ might want to	need to	ought to	won't	would

1. OK, let's move on. Now I want to look at different ways we'll be conserving energy in the future. (**a**) <u>I advise you to</u> move to the front so you can see the screen. (**b**) <u>Somebody</u> turn the lights off, please. (**c**) Um, <u>it's necessary for me to</u> find the clip on the computer. (**d**) <u>I believe it's</u> on my desktop. (**e**) Oh, <u>it's failing to</u> open. I'll go onto the next one.

a. You might want to move to the front so you can see the screen.
b. _____
c. _____
d. _____
e. _____

can	had better	might want to	should	will

2. (**a**) <u>Is everyone able to</u> see the chart on page 2 of the handout? (**b**) <u>I believe everyone has</u> a handout by now. (**c**) I can't explain these numbers in detail today, but <u>I advise you to</u> look up the information on our website. (**d**) If no one has any questions, <u>I'm offering to</u> give you a few more resources. (**e**) Then <u>it's necessary for us to</u> stop.

a. _____
b. _____
c. _____
d. _____
e. _____

Lesson C Conversation strategies

A Check (✔) the places where you can add one of the softening expressions in the box.

I would say / I'd say	I would think / I'd think	I would imagine / I'd imagine

Isabella Wow, ☐ did you hear? The *Times-Journal* is going paperless.

Sou-Chun Yeah, no more actual newspaper. You know, ☐ all newspapers are going to be doing this in the near future, fortunately.

Isabella I suppose. Though ☐ a lot of people still like to hold a real newspaper in their hands. For example, ☐ my mom says she gets headaches when she reads on a screen.

Sou-Chun Really? I prefer the online versions. But ☐ reading on a screen will get easier pretty soon. You know, ☐ screen technology will probably get more advanced.

Isabella ☐ I hope you're right. But ☐ in the end, people will support anything that's better for the environment.

Sou-Chun Exactly. And it's cleaner – ☐ newspapers always get my hands dirty!

B Circle the best expressions to complete the conversations.

1. *A* What if all doctors could treat patients over the Internet? I mean, do you think that we'll all eventually be treated online – like, without seeing a real doctor?

    B **I don't think so. / I hope so.** There are a lot of illnesses that need the personal attention of a doctor.

2. *A* I get all my news from the Internet. I haven't read a newspaper in ages – and I don't miss it.

    B So, do you think that newspapers will all be online soon?

    A **I guess so. / I hope not.** Newspapers are struggling. Don't you think they'll eventually die out?

    B **I hope so. / I hope not.** I'll always want the *option* of reading a real newspaper.

3. *A* Do you think people will play more virtual-reality sports in the future?

    B **I guess so. / I hope not.** But they'll still play sports with their friends. It's a social thing.

    A But it can still be a social thing if you play with friends online.

    B Yes, but it's not the same as getting together, say in a park, and playing baseball or something.

    A **I guess not. / I think so.** Being outside is part of the fun.

4. *A* I heard that a restaurant near here is going to have tablets on every table. So we'll be ordering food without the waiter. Do you think that'll catch on?

    B Oh, **I hope so. / I guess not.** That'd be fun. It'd probably be quicker, too!

C Circle the best expressions. Then write softening expressions to complete the conversation. There may be more than one possible expression you can use.

A There are so many people with e-readers now! Do you think books will disappear completely?

B **I hope not. / I guess not.** I'm not ready to read everything on a screen.

A Yeah, but _____ e-readers are more practical. Think of all the books you can carry around!

B **I hope so. / I guess so.** I wonder if the screens will become interactive, like if you could talk to them or something. That would make it quicker to find things.

A _____ they will. I mean, computers and tablets are getting more interactive, so _____ the same will happen with e-readers, too.

A **Read for main ideas** Read the report from a conference on future technological challenges. Then write the correct headings in the report. There are three extra headings.

clean energy	communication	public health
clean water	poverty	public housing

Future technological challenges

1 As the world's population grows, one of the most difficult challenges we face is to improve our quality of life. Clean energy, disease prevention, and access to clean water are some of the most important aspects of this challenge, according to a group of leading experts at a recent world conference on technological advancement.

2 **1. _____**

Earth's growing population is consuming its resources too quickly, experts say. Scientists have emphasized the need to develop new sources of energy, while at the same time protecting the environment. Economists predict that oil prices will likely continue to rise, and consumers, especially large corporations, retailers, hospitals, and schools will be looking for cheaper sources of energy, such as solar power. The sun gives off more energy in one hour than the entire world population consumes in one year. However, the challenge for inventors is to convert solar power into useful forms, and to store it inexpensively.

3 **2. _____**

As more and more people live longer, there will be a greater demand for medical treatments that are effective, cheap, and available to everyone. Scientists are finding new ways to understand how the body works, and this new understanding could well lead to more personalized treatment. Personalized medicine will undoubtedly have enormous benefits to public health because it will help doctors and therapists to identify a patient's health problems earlier and treat them successfully. This should also reduce medical costs to patients.

4 **3. _____**

Climatologists and ecologists predict that a change in weather patterns will inevitably affect the planet in significant ways. Some areas will likely experience severe droughts, whereas others will see heavy flooding. Drought and floods can both lead to a shortage of clean drinking water and food and create an increase in refugees and migrants as people move to new areas in search of food or clean water. More investment in new technologies will undoubtedly be needed to make water safer in difficult times.

5 The above challenges cannot be met without economic support. All too often, cheaper technologies that pollute the environment are still preferred over cleaner, more expensive ones. On the last day of the conference, one expert concluded by saying, "If industries and governments don't invest in new technologies, we're going to destroy our planet and the people who live here. Earth's resources won't last forever and we might well become victims of our own lack of planning. Spending millions now might well save billions later."

B **Check your understanding** Answer the questions. Check (✔) a, b, or c.

1. What was the main theme of the recent conference?
   - ☐ a. finding ways to stop the population growing
   - ☐ b. improving the quality of life for people
   - ☐ c. sharing technologies

2. According to the report, what is one of the biggest challenges in using solar power?
   - ☐ a. There is not enough for our needs.
   - ☐ b. It is not environmentally friendly.
   - ☐ c. It is expensive to store.

3. What is one of the benefits of personalized medicine?
   - ☐ a. Treatment will be shorter.
   - ☐ b. Patients will have more access to treatment.
   - ☐ c. Treatment will be less expensive.

4. Which of these is not mentioned in the report as a result of the effects of climate change?
   - ☐ a. Areas will experience water shortages.
   - ☐ b. Rain will become more polluted.
   - ☐ c. People will have to leave their homes.

5. What is needed to meet the three challenges in the future, according to the report?
   - ☐ a. more inventors
   - ☐ b. less spending by governments
   - ☐ c. more investment in technology

C **Focus on vocabulary** Complete the definitions with words from the report.

1. _____ study the distribution of resources and the production of goods and services. (para. 2)
2. _____ sell things, and _____ buy them. (para. 2)
3. _____ create or design new things. (para. 2)
4. Doctors and _____ treat people with health problems. (para. 3)
5. _____ study weather and climate. (para. 4)
6. _____ study the natural relationships between the air, land, water, animals, plants, etc. (para. 4)
7. _____ go to other places or countries because they are escaping from a dangerous situation. (para. 4)
8. _____ are people who go to live in another place or country. (para. 4)
9. _____ are people who suffer the effects of something. (para. 5)

About you

D **Answer the question.**

One important message from the report is "You have to spend money to save money." Do you think this is true? Why or why not?

_____

_____

_____

_____

_____

_____

_____

_____

Writing A one-paragraph article

A Number the sections in the correct order to form a one-paragraph article. Then label the topic sentence (T), the supporting sentences (S), and the concluding sentence (C).

[ ] _____ Doctors and patients will benefit from these new technologies, which will undoubtedly make health care more effective and more convenient.

[ ] _____ New technology in medical care will undoubtedly give doctors more reliable information about a patient's health, and may well make visits to the doctor's office less frequent and possibly less unpleasant.

[ ] _____ Another exciting invention is a "pill-cam", a tiny wireless camera that patients swallow and which sends images of any health problems to their doctor's computer screen.

[ ] _____ One example of this technology is the "tele-health monitor". This piece of equipment, which patients will have in their homes, will constantly check a patient's health and send instant information to a doctor. When there is a problem, the doctor will call the patient immediately.

B Complete the article by adding the adverbs in parentheses.

                                                                     undoubtedly

    In the future, medical treatment, even in the poorest countries worldwide, will ∧ change to a system that starts before a patient gets sick. (undoubtedly) In the near future, doctors will be able to collect millions of pieces of information about a child shortly after birth. (likely) People will find out at an early stage if they will get sick in later life. (inevitably / eventually) However, with the kind of information that technology can give them, people may be able to take action to prevent illnesses until much later in their lives. (well) These advances will improve the quality of life and health of many people throughout their lives. (ultimately)

C Editing Complete the sentences with the adverbs in the box. Choose an adverb that adds the idea in parentheses. Sometimes more than one answer is possible.

actually	currently	eventually	maybe	recently	ultimately

1. Technology will _____ bring better treatments to everyone.
   (I'm sure this will happen in time.)
2. Doctors are _____ testing a new treatment for heart disease.
   (They are doing this now.)
3. The government has _____ invested in a hospital-building program.
   (They did this last year.)
4. Many people will _____ not want to know about their future health problems.
   (This is a fact.)
5. If technology develops, there will _____ be no human doctors.
   (This will happen in time.)
6. _____ in the future, we will be able to eradicate all disease.
   (I'm not 100 percent sure.)

D Write a one-paragraph article about a prediction for the future. Use the ideas above or your own ideas. Include a topic sentence, supporting sentences, and a concluding sentence. Then check your one paragraph article for errors.

Listening extra Challenges in the 21st century

A Write the captions in the boxes under the slides.

| Rising sea levels | The Arctic Ocean | The construction industry | Greenland |

1. 　☐ _____

2. 　☐ _____

3. 　☐ _____

4. 　☐ _____

B 📥 Listen to the lecture. Check (✔) the three topics in Exercise A that are included in the lecture.

C 📥 Listen again and complete the student's notes.

The 2007 United Nations study:

- estimated ocean levels would rise between _____ and _____ inches
  (= 18 to _____ centimeters)
- did not include the impact of _____ _____ – in particular in Greenland
  (then sea levels could rise by at least _____ _____, or 5 meters)

The new study from Norway estimates that:

- sea levels could rise by _____ feet (1.6 meters) by _____
- the Arctic Ocean will have _____ _____ during the summer

Talk will cover four impacts of rising sea levels:

1. Environmental impact – the effects on _____ and _____
2. Effect on climate – especially _____ and storms
3. Impact on _____ supplies
4. The _____ impacts, especially on _____ and fishing

About you

D Answer the questions about the information in the lecture.

1. Which information did you already know?

   _____

2. Did any information surprise you?

   _____

3. What other information have you read recently on this topic?

   _____

Progress charts

Unit 1 Progress chart

Mark the boxes to rate your progress.
☑ I can do it.   ? I can do it, but have questions.   ! I need to review it.
I can . . .

	To review, go back to these pages in the Student's Book.
☐ discuss friends, friendship, social networking, and compare networking habits.	12
☐ ask questions to get to know someone.	10
☐ use the present tense, *tend*, and *will* to talk about habits.	13
☐ describe people's personalities.	11
☐ ask questions to find out or check information.	14
☐ start questions with *And, But*, and *So* to link back to a previous speaker.	14
☐ use rising intonation to suggest answers to a question.	138
☐ write an argument using expressions like *whereas* to contrast ideas.	18

Unit 2 Progress chart

Mark the boxes to rate your progress.
☑ I can do it.   ? I can do it, but have questions.   ! I need to review it.
I can . . .

	To review, go back to these pages in the Student's Book.
☐ describe and give opinions on the impact of the media and celebrities.	20
☐ use defining and non-defining relative clauses to give and add information.	21
☐ use *that* clauses to link ideas.	23
☐ choose the correct preposition after at least 12 key nouns.	22
☐ use *which* clauses to comment on my own and other people's statements.	21
☐ use *You know what . . . ?* to introduce a comment on what I'm going to say.	25
☐ use falling intonation in *which* clauses.	138
☐ use a topic sentence in a paragraph and expressions like *First* to list ideas.	28

Unit 3 Progress chart

Mark the boxes to rate your progress.
☑ I can do it.   ? I can do it, but have questions.   ! I need to review it.
I can . . .

	To review, go back to these pages in the Student's Book.
☐ tell stories about my childhood, life experiences, and lessons learned.	34
☐ use the past tense and the present perfect to talk about the past.	31
☐ the simple past, past perfect, and past perfect continuous to sequence events.	33
☐ use at least 12 expressions to describe school-related experiences.	32
☐ interrupt a story I am telling to make a comment and then come back to it.	34
☐ use *(It's) no wonder* to say something is not surprising.	35
☐ reduce the auxiliary verbs *did* and *had*.	139
☐ write a narrative article using appropriate verb forms.	38

Unit 4 Progress chart

Mark the boxes to rate your progress. ☑ I can do it. ? I can do it, but have questions. !! I need to review it. I can . . .	To review, go back to these pages in the Student's Book.
☐ give advice on finding jobs and job interviews, and give opinions on benefits.	42
☐ identify and use countable and uncountable nouns correctly.	43
☐ use definite and indefinite articles to generalize and specify.	45
☐ use at least 12 verb + noun collocations on the topic of finding a job.	42
☐ use -ly adverbs to show my attitude toward what I say.	46
☐ use As a matter of fact or In fact to emphasize or correct information.	47
☐ stress the correct syllables in at least 15 words to talk about work.	139
☐ write a personal statement for an application using nouns instead of I + verb.	50

Unit 5 Progress chart

Mark the boxes to rate your progress. ☑ I can do it. ? I can do it, but have questions. !! I need to review it. I can . . .	To review, go back to these pages in the Student's Book.
☐ describe and give opinions on social problems, world issues and solutions.	54
☐ use conditional sentences to hypothesize about events in the present or past.	53
☐ use wish and hope to express wishes, hopes, and regrets.	55
☐ remember at least 12 words to talk about world problems and solutions.	54
☐ use What if . . . ?, suppose, and imagine to suggest possible scenarios or ideas.	56
☐ use I suppose to show that I'm not 100 percent sure.	57
☐ stress the correct syllables in different forms of 10 words for world issues.	140
☐ write an inquiry and use it as a subject or as an object.	60

Unit 6 Progress chart

Mark the boxes to rate your progress. ☑ I can do it. ? I can do it, but have questions. !! I need to review it. I can . . .	To review, go back to these pages in the Student's Book.
☐ talk about the future of money, technology, clothing, travel, and entertainment.	62
☐ use the present tense be going to, will, might, may to describe future events.	63
☐ use modal verbs for expectations, guesses, necessity, advice, requests, etc.	65
☐ remember at least 12 expressions to use when giving a presentation.	64
☐ use would or 'd to soften my opinions.	66
☐ use so in responses like I think so to avoid repeating words.	67
☐ pronounce at least 12 words with silent consonants.	140
☐ structure a paragraph and use modal verbs with adverbs, like will eventually.	70

Photography credits

2 Paul Bradbury/age fotostock
5 Suprijono Suharjoto/iStockphoto
6 *(woman)* age fotostock/SuperStock; *(background)* Neliyana Kostadinova/Shutterstock
8 Jared DeCinque/iStockphoto
9 *(left to right)* ostill/Shutterstock; Hongqi Zhang/iStockphoto; Justin Horrocks/iStockphoto; Supri Suharjoto/Shutterstock
11 Oleksiy Mark/Shutterstock
12 Andrea Danti/Shutterstock
14 CHASSENET/age fotostock
16 *(skateboarder)* Vladimir Ivanovich Danilov/Shutterstock; *(computer monitor)* Iakov Filimonov/Shutterstock; *(sample website)* Michael Monahan/Shutterstock
17 *(left to right)* Netfalls/Shutterstock; Rich Legg/iStockphoto; Jupiterimages/Thinkstock
19 Andy Cook/iStockphoto
21 Imagesource/Glow Images

22 *(boy)* Matthew Plexman/age fotostock; *(man)* Duncan Walker/iStockphoto; *(lion)* Kennan Ward/Corbis/Glow Images
24 Kuttig - Travel/Alamy
25 *(left to right)* Richard Semik/Shutterstock; ixer/Shutterstock; vilax/Shutterstock; Dima367/Dreamstime.com; IBI/Shutterstock
26 Dmitriy Shironosov/Shutterstock
28 Tom Mc Nemar/Shutterstock
33 Wavebreakmedia Ltd/Dreamstime
34 Gus Ruelas/AP Images
35 Jim West/Alamy
38 Claudia Dewald/iStockphoto
41 ©zhang bo/iStockphoto
42 Leslie Richard Jacobs/Corbis/Glow Images
43 *(woman)* Fancy/Veer/Corbis/Glow Images; *(globe)* Vasiliy Yakobchuk/iStockphoto
49 *(left to right)* Mlenny Photography/iStockphoto; Dawn Nichols/iStockphoto; Dmitry Skalev/iStockphoto; sculpies/iStockphoto

Text credits

Every effort has been made to trace the owners of copyrighted material in this book. We would be grateful to hear from anyone who recognizes his or her copyrighted material and who is unacknowledged. We will be pleased to make the necessary corrections in future editions of the book.

Corpus

Development of this publication has made use of the Cambridge English Corpus (CEC). The CEC is a computer database of contemporary spoken and written English, which currently stands at over one billion words. It includes British English, American English and other varieties of English. It also includes the Cambridge Learner Corpus, developed in collaboration with the University of Cambridge ESOL Examinations. Cambridge University Press has built up the CEC to provide evidence about language use that helps to produce better language teaching materials.